Jessie Louise Jones

The Phonology of the Elis Saga

Jessie Louise Jones

The Phonology of the Elis Saga

ISBN/EAN: 9783744779470

Printed in Europe, USA, Canada, Australia, Japan

Cover: Foto ©Thomas Meinert / pixelio.de

More available books at **www.hansebooks.com**

THE UNIVERSITY OF CHICAGO.

FOUNDED BY JOHN D. ROCKEFELLER.

THE PHONOLOGY

OF THE

ELIS SAGA

A DISSERTATION
SUBMITTED TO THE FACULTIES OF THE
GRADUATE SCHOOLS OF ARTS, LITERATURE, AND
SCIENCE, IN CANDIDACY FOR THE DEGREE OF
DOCTOR OF PHILOSOPHY.
DEPARTMENT OF GERMANIC LANGUAGES AND LITERATURES

BY

JESSIE LOUISE JONES

——— — —

CHICAGO

1897.

Printed by G. Otto, Darmstadt.

CONTENTS.

INTRODUCTION.

The Elis saga is the Old Norwegian version of the French chanson de geste, Elie de Saint Gille. The translation was made by the abbot Robert, at the direction of the king Hakon Hakonson, probably in the second quarter of the thirteenth century.

The principal manuscript is the one known as A, in the library of the University of Upsala. The only edition of the saga is that of Eugen Kölbing, Heilbronn, 1881, upon which the present work on the phonology is based. In the introduction to this edition is found a full discussion of the manuscript question.

The principal French manuscript is fr. 25 516 in the Bibliothèque Nationale ed. by Gaston Raynaud, Paris, 1879. This is also a copy or version, made in the thirteenth century, of an older work. The original, upon which both French and Norwegian versions are based, dates, probably, from the twelfth century.

ABBREVIATIONS.

Ark.	= Arkiv för Nordisk Filologi.
B.	= Beiträge zur Geschichte der deutschen Sprache und Literatur, herausgegeben von H. Paul und W. Braune.
Barl.	= Barlaams ok Josaphats saga, Keyser and Unger. Christiania, 1851.
El.	= Elis saga ok Rosamundu, Eugen Kölbing. Heilbronn, 1881.
Fritzner	Fritzner, Ordbog over det Gamle Norske Sprog. Kristiania, 1883.
Grd.	Paul's Grundriss der germanischen Philologie.
Hom. Ll.	= Homiliebokens Ljudlära. Elis Wadstein, Upsala, 1890.
Kahle	= Altisländisches Elementarbuch, Heidelberg, 1896.
Kluge	= Kluge's Etymologisches Wörterbuch.
Lit. Zt.	= Litteratur-Zeitung.
Noreen Gr.	= Altisländische und Altnorwegische Grammatik. Adolf Noreen, Halle 1892.
Skr. Hum. Vet.	= Skrifter utgifna af Humanistiska Vetenskapssamfundet i Upsala.
Sv. Lm.	= Bidrag till kännedom om de Svenska Landsmålen ock Svenskt Folklif.
Tüb. Br.	= Tübinger Bruchstücke der älteren Frostuthingslög, E. Sievers.

Letters italicized in the text of Kölbing, to indicate the abbreviations of the ms., are enclosed in parenthesis.

t. = times, m. t. = many times.

PHONOLOGY.

PART I

VOWELS.

CHAPTER I.

VOWELS IN SYLLABLES WITH CHIEF ACCENT AND STRONG SECONDARY ACCENT.

§ 1. Germanic *a*

1) = *a*, *c. g. barns* 23[7], *bar* 35[15], *gras* 32[3].
2)) *á* (usually written without accent):
    a) When final, *c. g. á* (prep.) 5[14], *bra* 32[1].
    b) By compensatory lengthening; *c.g. ass* 12[8], *mál* 23[7].
    c) Before consonant combinations: before *tt* (*ht*), *c.g. mattugr* 72[7]; before cacuminal *l* - - consonant, *c. g. hálsi* 42[7]. According to Noreen, Gr., § 111, 3., a. 3., this lengthening is rare in Norwegian dialects.

    Since the quantity of the vowels is for the most part not indicated in El. this question cannot be determined with certainty. However the accent, when it is used, usually marks a long vowel (cf. Chapter III), so it is probable that this is a case of such lengthening. The example given is the only case where the accent is written. Other examples without sign of lengthening are: forms of *halfr*, *c. g.* 78[7], forms of *hialpa*, *c. g.* 70[10], forms of *hialmr*, *c. g.* 101[5]. Wadstein, Hom. Ll., p. 121, gives several instances of such lengthening in Hom.

Note. In a foot-note on the page referred to, Wadstein suggests, that, as the only Modern Norwegian dialects where this lengthening is known are Saetersdalen and Telmarken, the presence of a few such cases in Hom. might

indicate that the ms. originated in one of those places. With equal reason
we might refer the ms. of El. to one of these places.

2) *e* by *i*-umlaut.

The regular representation of this umlaut in El. is *e*; *e. g.*
bernskr 15[10], forms of *brenna*, *e. g.* 80[4], *degi* 8 t. *e. g.* 12[1], *gengit*
80[13], *hendr* 10 t. *e. g.* 94[2]. It is also represented by *æ* 13 times,
as follows: forms of *ællztr* 38[4], 78[15], forms of *ærfd* 8[14], 4[9]
(∼ *erfda* 1[10]), *ærfingi* 3[1], *ændilongu* 31[1] (∼ *endilongu* 112[5],
enda 30[11]), *æfter* 26[13], 41[14] (*pt*), (∼ *eftir* 15t. *e. g.* 80[10]), *hæfer*
(*hafa*) 23[7] (∼ forms of *hava* with *e.* m. t. *e. g.* 70[1]), *ælli* 3[6],
ængiar 34[3], -*om* 36[17] (∼ *engium* 78[3], 23[13]).

This *e*) *œ* by *w*-umlaut: *e. g.* *œxi* 37[11], 73[3].

4) *o* (*au*) by *u*-umlaut:
    a) When the umlaut-producing *u* has been lost.
       110 cases occur in El. where *a* was followed by
       an *u* which has disappeared. In all of these
       cases umlaut occurs: *bond* (n. pl.) 5 t. *e. g.* 30[14],
       38[6], *fogr* (n. s. f.) 33[11], 74[4], *hond* 10 t. *e. g.* 30[14].
    b) When the umlaut-producing *u* remains. Of 247
       cases occurring with *u* retained after *a*, 236 have
       umlaut and 11 do not. Examples with umlaut
       are: *ollu* 12 t. *e. g.* 6[4], 7[9] (*aullu* 3 t. *e. g.* 24[12]),
       ollum 17 t. *e. g.* 110[12], 113[1], (*aullum* 6 t. *e. g.*
       93[8]), *fogrum* 34[3], 95[11] (*faugrom* 72[4]), *gaungom*
       20[8], *hongu* 77[8], *hvossum* 43[3], *saumu* 8[6]. *saumu* is
       corrected to *sann* by Cederschiöld, Lit. Zt. III 14. col. 502.

       The 11 cases without umlaut are as follows:
       havom 20[3], 62[3] (∼ *hovum* 20[5], 38[5]), *akavom* 5[3],
       ambun 25[6], *ambuna* 6[5] (∼ *au*(*m*)*bun* 109[14]), *al-*
       mosor 2[3], 3[5], *kastalum* 68[15], *spitalum* 2[2], *skinandom*
       87[4], *biorblandodu* 61[1].

The question as to the *u*-umlaut of *a* in the Norse languages
has received much attention of late, two theories having come
into especial prominence, namely, those of Axel Kock and Elis
Wadstein. The literature bearing on the two theories just
named is as follows: Kock, Ark., IV, X, XII, and B., XIV,
Svenska Landsmål, XII; Wadstein, B, XVII, Sv. Lm., XIII,
Skr. Hum. Vet., III., Hum. Ll., pp. 42 ff., 142.

Kock's theory is, in brief, that there were two periods of *u*-umlaut, an earlier one, in which umlaut was produced only by syncopated *u*, and a later one, in which umlaut was produced by *u* preserved, the second period having affected only the Icelandic and certain Norwegian dialects.

Wadstein's theory assumes that there was a general extension of the umlaut, produced both by syncopated and retained *u*, its non-appearance in Danish, O. Swedish and some Norwegian dialects being due to the interference of certain consonants.

Neither theory is in all respects satisfactory, but of the two, Kock's is simpler and covers more cases. A considerable number of words with umlaut in O. Sw. and in those Norw. dialects which do not, in general, have umlaut are explained by Kock as being influenced by a second factor besides the *u*, that is, a labial consonant or a nasal — the so-called combined umlaut.

The umlaut in El. is satisfactorily explained in accordance with the theory of two umlaut periods. The cases of umlaut mentioned above show that the later umlaut, as well as the earlier, has prevailed in this dialect. The eleven exceptions may be explained as follows: *harom*, twice, (~ *horom* twice), must have occurred very frequently without accent in the sentence, in which case the vowel would not be umlauted. *akarom* is due to analogy from the cases where *a* is regular. *ambun*, *ambuna* (~ *aumbun* once). — This word occurs with suffix -*an* as well as -*un*. The umlauted vowel regular with the latter suffix could easily appear in the other form. *almoser*, twice. — This word occurs with and without umlaut in Icelandic it may be due to variation in accent; with fortis on the penult the *u* would produce no umlaut. *kastalum*, *spitalum*. — These are loan-words. Perhaps the accent was on the first syllable. *skinandom*, — due either to analogy or to weak accent of syllable -*an*. *biorblandodn*. This is due to the analogy of forms where *a* is regular. The wavering of *a o* in unaccented syllables as a representative of *ǫ* is characteristic of Norwegian dialects (cf. Noreen, Gr., § 117, a. 3), and is especially frequent in this ms. (s. p. 15). This very word occurs with *a*, *samblandadum* 27. This would cause a variation in the preceding vowel.

1*

The signs used to represent this umlaut are *o*, *au*, *oe* (once). They are distributed as follows: earlier umlaut 89 *o* ⁓ 23 *au*, later umlaut 143 *o* ⁓ 112 *au*. *au* undoubtedly represents a more open sound, and since it occurs so much more frequently in the case of the later umlaut it is probable that this umlaut was of a different nature. In the case of the *w*-umlaut also, which was produced whether *w* dropped out or remained, *o* is used 46 times when *w* is lost, and *au* only 16 times; while, when *w* is retained, we have 7 t. *au* ⁓ 13 t. *o* - a larger proportion. This is perhaps a slight confirmation of the theory of two periods.

The single instance of *oe* for this umlaut, *roeddo* 25[9] (⁓ *roddu'o* 9 t. *e. g.* 29[1]), is due to dittography: *"pa oepti ha(nn) harri roeddo"*.

furu madr 62[15] is, according to Fritzner, a mistake for *foru-*.

5) *: o* (*au*) by *w*-umlaut.

As mentioned in 4), umlaut is here produced, whether *w* fell out or was retained; *e. g. daugurd* 60[15], forms of *gorr* (*gera*) 17 t. *e. g.* 8[10], forms of *nockorr* 17 t. *e. g.* 89 [7], 106[7], forms of *bolva* 10 t. *e. g.* 72[1], *bolui* 34[10] ⁓ *boelvi* 33[16]. In the latter form we have perhaps the *i*-uml. of *ǫ* (cf. Noreen, Gr., § 72, a. 8.). In *bolui o* is restored after the analogy of the numerous forms of this word with *o*. *Valslongur* 78[4] may be either *w*-umlaut or younger *u*-umlaut. *natt-songi* 12[6] (n. sg.) has umlaut from the analogy of *songr*. (This word is given neither by Fritzner nor Vigf. as a weak noun.)

6) is written *ae* in *faengs* 20[5]. This is due to dittography, *"gaeta faengs"*.

§ 2. Germanic *e*

1) = *e*: In forms of *bera* m. t. *e. g.* 81[18], *lesa* 7[2], *med* (prep.) 37[12]. *e* is the regular representative of Germanic *e*; yet *ae* occurs in *ofmaetnadr* 88[1] (⁓ forms of *metnadr* 8 t. *e. g.* 27[2]), *vaerit* (ppl. of *vera*) 64[11] ⁓ *verit* 64[11], 74[16] — also for Latin *e* in the loan-word *bracvi* 78[6].

2) *é*: *fé* (simple and in cpds.) 18 t. *e. g.* 20[4], 69[16], *fletingu(m)* 95[11] (cf. *flaettingu(m)* 87[4]), *kné* 64[3], 65[3], *sé* (*sjá*) 6[6].

3) *ea* *ia* by *a*-breaking; *i. g. biargar* (g. s.) 22⁹,
forms of *biarga* (vb.) 37¹⁰, 38¹³, forms of *diarfr* 14 t.
e. g. 19⁹, *fiarreli* (adv.) 11 t. *e. g.* 28¹⁵, *giarn(n)a*
(adv.) 6 t. *e. g.* 31¹⁵.

4) *eo* *io* by *n*-breaking:

a) When *u* is lost: *fiöldi* 36¹², 40⁷, 116¹, *giof*
34⁶, 88¹¹, *-giord* 87², *hiolp* (n. a. s.) 6 t. *e. g.*
31³ (∼ *hialp* (a. s.) 89¹³ with *a* by analogy from
other cases), *iord* 98¹, *mioc* 26 t. *e. g.* 3⁸, *miod-*
75⁹, *skiolldr* 9¹⁰, 44¹³, *skiolld* (a. s.) 14 t. *e. g.*
33², *-tiolld* 78⁸.

b) With *u* retained: *giognum* 7 t. *e. g.* 16¹² ∼
gegnum 13⁷, 25¹⁵, *giegnum* 60¹¹. Of these
forms *giognum* is the form which arose when the
word had the chief accent, *gegnum* was the proclitic form, cf. Noreen, Gr., § 71, a. 2., *giegnum*,
has *i* inserted after the analogy of *giognum*.
hioltum 3 t. *e. g.* 98⁸, *jorlu* (d. pl.) 36¹ᶜ, 42¹¹,
iordu (d. s.) 3 t. *e. g.* 13 ¹, *miorkui* 68² (∼
moerkui 70⁴), *skiolldu um* 7 t. *e. g.* 6², *siolfum*
75¹³ ∼ *sialvum'om* 6 t. (*a* by analogy).

The above examples confirm the later view of
Noreen, explained by Wadstein, Hom Ll., p. 63,
that *e* is broken to *io* not *iø* when *u* follows, for
the sign *au*, which is so frequently used for the
umlaut of *a* (i. e. *ǫ*), does not occur here in a
single instance.

5) Forms of *gera:* — Since Germ. *e* and umlaut-*e* are represented by the same letter, it is impossible to tell,
from this ms., whether the stem vowel is Germ. *e*, as
Wadstein suggests in Hom. Ll., p. 54. The forms of
the ppl. are all written with *o*, 16 t. *e. g.* 31 ¹², which
points to a stem vowel *a*, at least in the ppl. The
following derivatives have *o:* forms of *ogorligr* 3 t.
e. g. 96¹², *gorl.r* 74¹⁵, *giorsamliga* 62⁴, *stilgorvan* 101⁴.
If the stem vowel is *e*, then *giorsamliga* is the broken
vowel, but if the stem is *a*, there is an insertion
of *i* before a non-palatal vowel (cf. other ex. p. 23).

6) *œ* by *æ*-umlaut: *e. g. mœrkui* 70[1], (cf. *miorkui* 68[2], forms of *myrkva* 3 t. *e. g.* 72[12]).

These forms represent three different developments of Germ. *e*: (1) *e* *œ* by *æ*-umlaut, (2) *e* *io* by *u*- or *w*-breaking, (3) *e* *i* in urgerm., *y* by *æ*-umlaut. By leveling all these forms occur in the noun.

7) *j*: in *fiar* 7[3], 64[5], forms of *sia, e. g.* 110[11].

8) *fiell* 35[17] (pret. of *falla*) is certainly after the analogy of *kiendi* etc., (see p. 23).

§ 3. Germanic *i*

1) — *i*:
binda, e.g. 39[6], forms of *bidia, e.g.* 6[12], *innan* (adv.) 4 t. *e. g.* 11[8].

2) *e* when a nasal has been lost:
Forms of *brekka* 3 t. *e. g.* 27[2], *drecka* 33[12], 75[14], *geck* 14 t. *e. g.* 104[4] (cf. *gek* 97[7]), *vetr* 3[2].

3) *y* by *æ*-umlaut:
Forms of (*h*)*ryggr* (adj.), *e. g.* 74[1], *syngia* 7[2], 72[4], *tryguan* 115[14], *ykr* (pron.) 3 t. *e. g.* 42[8].

4) *y* by combined *u*-umlaut, *i. e.*, after *m*, cf. Noreen, Gr., § 74. Forms of *mikill* with *u* in the ending have *y* 5 t. *e. g. Mycklu* 90[9] ∼ *i* 20 t. *e. g. micklu* 81[12]. The *i* is due to leveling. In forms without *u* in the ending *y* has crowded in, in *mykill* 4[1], *myckla* 104[12].

5) *ui* *y* by *u*-umlaut:
Forms of *kyrr* 6 t. *e. g.* 3[4], *systur* 5 t. *e. g.* 24[11]. This umlaut does not appear in *suikum* 101[8] and *suikull* 99[13].

6) — *y* in *gymstacinu*(*m*) 115[2] ∼ (*gim-* 86[13]). This is a change which occurs sporadically in Old Norwegian. Cf. Noreen, Gr., § 74.

7) = *e* in *sec* 76[1], 84[11] (∼ *sik* 7 t. *e. g.* 39[3]), *þek* 4 t. *e.g.* 88[9] (∼ *þik* 22 t. *e. g.* 109[13]). The *e* in these forms may be due to the *e*-vowel in nominative and dative. Cf. Hom. Ll., p. 53.

§ 4. Germanic *o*

1) — *o*: Forms of *koma, e. g.* 18[14], *spotti* 12[12].

2) *ó*:
a) When final: *e. g.* in *lo* (*h*)*lacia*) 11[7].

b) Before cacuminal *l* - consonant(?), *folki* 22³, forms of *golf* 5¹, 103⁸. This is uncertain, since this vowel is not marked by an accent.

3) *œ* by *i*-umlaut:
In forms of *koma* 12 t. *c. g. kœmr* 7¹³ (~ forms with *e* 2 t. *kemr* 41¹², *kemz* 36ᵇ), *œfre* 14⁶, *œrua* 8¹, *-it* 115¹¹.
For the variation of *œ/e* cf. Noreen, Gr., § 86. ¹
This umlaut is written *ø* occasionally; *c.g.* in *sǿfr* 98¹¹.
In the preterite subjunctive of *munu* forms with *œ* occur twice 5⁷, 37⁹, forms with *ø* once, *mǿnda* 81¹⁰, forms with *y* 12 t. *c. g.* 67⁷, forms with *u* twice 98⁸. 110¹⁴. These forms are confused on account of the variation of *ø u* in the stem. *mœyndi* 74¹ has *œ* inserted by dittography "ef hann saei hana. þa *mœyndi* hann."
In the forms of *haversklavik, a* is written for *œ: hav(er)-sclaviks* 1ⁿ, *haverklavik* 86⁴, *haverskd* 22⁴. Cf. Fritzner.

4) *œ* in *nœrrœun* 116⁹. This is undoubtedly due to anticipation by the copyist of the *œ* in the second syllable.

5) Latin *o* is represented in some words by *u*: In forms of *munkr, c. g.* 46⁶, *mustri* 17¹³.

§ 5. Germanic *u*

1) *u*: Examples are: *kunnu* 98¹², forms of *sunr* 5 t. *c. g.* 4¹³ (~ forms with *o* 22 t.). Double forms with *o u* arose from the variation of *u o* in Pregermanic.
Forms of *uruggr* occur 4 t. with *u, c. g.* 5¹³ ~ forms with *au* 2 t. 96³, 114¹². If the etymology given by Vigfusson is correct (*ur-uggr* [danger¹]), this prefix corresponds to Gothic *uz*. We should expect *u o u* by *R*-umlaut. The *u* may, however, be due to the proclitic position of the word as prefix.

2) *u* when final: *nu* (adv.) m. t. *c. g.* 14⁹.

3) *ð*:
a) Before a nasal which has disappeared, *c. g. o*, the neg. prefix, in which *u* and *o* vary according to the accent. *o* occurs 42 t. ~ *u* 9 t. *c. g. ogaefu*

¹) *œ* is *ø* in the ms. Cf. El. Einleitung p. XXXVI

79[6]. Further examples are: *oss* (pers. pron.) m. t. *c.g.* 18[5], forms of *okkarr* (pers. pron.) 3 t. *c.g.* 9[8].

b) Before *tt* (*ht*): Forms of *dottir* 14 t. *c.g.* 89[10], *drottin* 11 t. *c.g.* 8[12].

4) ⟩ *r* by *i*-umlaut: Forms of *brynia* 22 t. *c.g.* 23[5], *hrygdar* 84[14], *dryckit* 75[15] ~ *druckit* 76[7] (sup.).

The umlaut in *dryckit* is irregular. Perhaps it is from analogy to the noun *dryckr*, which follows in the same sentence. We should expect *o* instead of *u* in *druckit*, before the nasal, but *u* has been restored by leveling.

5) In the forms of *munu*, *a* stands for Germ. *u̯o* in sg. *man* 67[6], 81[3] (~ *mon* 19 t. *c. g.* 22[5]).

6) Irregular representations of Germ. *u*. *hvglaeysi* 27[12], due to confusion with consonantal *u*, cf. *hyglaeysi* 81[7] (uml. by analogy). *flogskiota* 81[7] has *o* due to careless writing after *o* in the second syllable. *fullnomi* 1[8] is probably due to careless writing. (*fullnomsi* occurs once in Barl., cf. Fritz. and Vigf.)

§ 6.   Germanic •*a* (*anχ*)

1) = *á*: *fa* 10 t. *c. g.* 78[12].

2) ⟩ *ae* by *i*-umlaut: *faer* 5 t. *c.g.* 4[15] (possibly *R*-umlaut), forms of *gaeta*, *c. g.* 15[7], forms of *raena*, *c.g.* 60[12] (O. H. G. *bi-rahanen*). The ppl. of *raena*, *renntir* 1[10] has *e* for *ae*.

3) ⟩ *ae* by *R*-umlaut, *e. g.* *þaer* 39[11], 61[10] The *á* in this word has arisen through secondary lengthening of unaccented *þaR cf. Noreen, Grd., p. 501. Once *e* is written for *ae*, in *þer* 86[11]. It is not strange that *e* is used for *ae*, since both signs are used to represent Germanic *e* and umlaut-*e*.

§ 7. Germanic *ē*

1) = *á*: *c.g.* *blasa* 13[5], forms of *manadr*, *c. g.* 38[4], *sua* (adv.) *c. g.* 1[4].

2) ⟩ *ae* by *i*-umlaut, *e.g.* *draepi* 95[8], *saeti* 5[8]. This *ae* and the one arising from § 6, 2) may be further palatalized to *e* before *R*, see Kock, Ark., XIII, p. 167.

The orthography of this ms. confirms Kock's theory. The adv. *naer* 69[5] occurs also as *ner* 98[1], 35[5].

The superlative, which has its vowel from analogy to the comparative, is written *naestur* 103[11], *nestur* 36[13]. Furthermore the adverb *nest* occurs 19 t. with *e*, but always in the combination *fur nest*, where it may be explained as having a secondary accent and, consequently, reduction of vowel. Other forms occurring in the ms. showing this somewhat rare combination, which might support the theory, are *faer* (see § 6. 2) and *naer* (3 s. *na*) 112[1]; but these are here written with *ae*.

3) *ae* by *R*-umlaut; e. g. *gaerkuelld* 73[4] ∼ *giarkuelld* 99[12]. The form *giar* is probably analogy from O. Swed. The regular form in O. Swed. is *gar* without umlaut. *i* is an insertion before a non-palatal vowel, cf. Noreen, Gr.[1], § 226 a. 4. *maer* m. t. e. g. 70[4].

4) The *ae* in § 7, 2) may be *u*-umlauted to *oe*, cf. Noreen, Gr., § 71, a. 2. Probably the *oe* in forms of *oerendi* 3 t. e. g. 78[6], is of this sort, the *u*-umlaut having arisen from a contamination of the suffixes *-und*, *-ind*. Cf. Noreen, Gr., § 149, 3, § 150, 2.

5) *o* by *u*-umlaut: e. g. *kuodu* 43[15], *von* 4 t. e. g. 9[8]. In the great majority of cases *a* appears for this umlaut: *badom* (d. pl.) 4 t. e. g. 66[4], *drapu o* 3 t. e. g. 18[6], *sarom* 3 t. e. g. 74[13], *vafu* 86 , *fradum* 86[10].

Since the use of *a* for this umlaut is so general, the supposition arises: (1) either that *a* was not umlauted at all in this dialect, or (2) that *ǫ* has fallen together with *a* and is represented by the latter sign, as was the case in Icelandic after 1250 (cf. Noreen, Gr. § 80). The former supposition is very improbable since the two periods of umlaut of *a* have prevailed. The objection to the second supposition is, that in certain cases, where the regular development in East as well as West Norse is from *ǫ o*, we find here also *a*. The cases in which *a* before an *u* following is further labialized to *o* are as follows: (1) when preceded by *v*; (2) when nasalized, cf. Noreen, Gr., § 73, 2, Hom. Ll., pp. 66 ff.

1. Preceded by *v*. All the cases in El. where these conditions appear are as follows: *huar* (n. s. f.) 65[8], *kuad* 32[16]

(cf. *knodu* 43[15]), *samknomn* 89[9], 108[6], *vafn* 86[9], *valkum* 12[1], *vafn* 5 t. *c. g.* 3[3], *vapnom'um* 10 t. *c. g.* 4[11], *vár* (poss. n. pl.) 20[6], *varo* 7[3], 01[13], *varom* 8 t. *c. g.* 109[5], *vorum* 27[7], forms of *vera*: *varom* 18[1], *varo* 11 t. *c. g.* 43[6], *voru/o* 24 t. *c. g.* 103[11], *vorot* 94[1]. Of the above 71 forms, 29 have *o* and 42 *a*.

2. Nasalized: in *ast* 76[6], 91[17], *blam* (d. pl.) 26[6], *mattu* (*mega*) 36[12], 41[9], 68[3], forms of *mattngr* 9 t. *c. g.* 60[6], 83[2], *namo* 42[4], *nott* 6 t. *c. g.* 71[17], *on* (prep.) 4 t. *c. g.* 62[10], *asiandom* 35[18], *vún* 4 t. *c. g.* 21[9] (perhaps *monu* 37[5], 68[5]). Of the above 31 forms 14 have *o*, the rest *a*. [1]

> [1] Included in the above examples are all *á*'s, whatever their origin.

There are a few other words which must be mentioned in this connection, namely:

forsio 3 t. *c. g.* 1[3], *hon* 57 t. *c. g.* 60[1], *honum/om* 135 t. *c. g.* 44[4], *sniorr* 73[14], 95[10]. In some of these it is not absolutely certain that the original vowel was *á*. Cf. Hom. Ll., p. 64, and Kahle, § 73, 2. They are therefore disregarded in discussing the umlaut of *á*.

From the evidence of El. it appears that the development was not to *ó*, but simply to *ǫ* in these cases. On this supposition the wavering between *a* and *o* is explained, for it was approximately at the date of this ms. that the change took place. It will be noticed, also, that in every case where it is preceded by *v*, the *v* is retained, which would not be the case if we had *ó*. Although the ms. offers no examples of *v* dropped before *ó*, yet we may be sure it would drop in this case, since it is regularly dropped before *ǫ* and *u*.

This dialect certainly occupies a peculiar position in this respect, since the evidence for *ó* in most dialects seems very strong. Cf. Wadstein and Noreen, as above.

§ 8. Germanic *ē*

— *e*: e.g. *lezk* 82[1] (cf. *laétk* 81[6]), *her* (adv.) 7[3] etc.

In *laétk* (see above), in *vaer* 47 t. *c. g.* 8[6] (with accent 18[1]), (cf. *ver* 8[6]), *ae* is used to represent this *e*. This is remarkable. *e   ae* when preceded by *v* and followed by *r* or *l* in many Norwegian dialects, cf. Noreen, Gr., § 81, and Hom. Ll., p. 56 but no instance is recorded of a similar change of *é*. These are the only cases in this ms.

§ 9. Germanic *i*

1) = *i*: *c. g. bita* 30[13], forms of *rıkr c g.* 7[8].

2) *i* before *h*: *c. g. li* 22[15], *tuefallda* 13[7] (*tænk*) Noreen, Gr., § 251, a.

3) *i*: *c. g. tia* 82[3], *hia* (*heiwa*) 11 t. *c. g.* 76[13].

§ 10. Germanic *o*

1) — *o*: — *c. g. blod* 106[2], *godum* 102[8], *for* 111[9].

2) *oe* (*ø*) by *i*-umlaut: *c. g. bœnir* 3[5], 12[5], *brøðr* 5 t. *c. g.* 30[7], *fœti* 6 t. *c. g.* 7[7] (cf. *føti* 97[2]), forms of *rœda* 3 t. with *oe*, *c. g.* 82[10] ~ 14 t. with *ø*, *c. g. røðer* 32[10], *sœti* 91[16]. *oe* is used altogether 97 times, *ø* 48 times.

§ 11. Germanic *u*

1) = *u*: *bua* 6 t. *c. g.* 114[12], *hus* 109[11].

2) *y* by *i*-umlaut: *c. g. byr* 77[1], *bylr* 115[8], *suyr* 108[5].

3) *ǿ* before *h*. This *ǿ* *oe* by *i*-umlaut: *c. g. oesku* 1[7], 3[6], 91[16], *øsca* 106[10].

§ 12. Germanic *ai*

1) — *aei*: *c. g. aeiga* 7[10]. 99[1], *graeip* 5 t. *c. g* 7[11]. The usual representation of this diphthong is *aei*, but *ei* occurs in the following cases: *eigi* 60[16] (~ *aeigi* 95 t. *c. g.* 65[8]), *einnigi* 88[2] (~ forms with *aei* 8 t. *c. g.* 80[12]).

2) *e* by shortening before geminata: forms of *helgr* 15 t. *c. g.* 17[10] (~ *haelgar* 3[5], *iartegnir* 45[1] (cf. Hom. l.l., p. 60 for etymology), forms of *mestr* 7 t. *c. g.* 74[13].

3) *a*:

a) Before *h*; *c. g. a* (*eiga*) 4[15], *lain* 7[11].

b) Before *r*; *arla* (adv.) 3 t. *c. g.* 27[6], forms of *sar*, *c. g.* 81[12].

c) Before *w*; *c. g.* forms of *sal* 98[11], 22[7], *aei* (Goth. *aiw*) remains, cf. Noreen, Gr., § 57, 3. a. 2. It occurs 7 t. *c. g.* 16[6] (~ *ae* 83[5]).

d) In syllables with strong secondary accent, originally, and thence in syllables with chief accent: forms of *baðir c. g.* 26[2], forms of *klaedi* (*i*-uml.) *c. g.* 86[10].

§ 13. Germanic *au*

1)   *au*: forms of *daudr*, c. g. 66[7], *skaut* (*skjota*)
     7 t. c. g. 25[5], (*au* 66[13]), *þau* 9 t. c. g. 43[7].

2)   *aey* by *i*-umlaut: c. g. *daeyia* 106[10], *kaeyfti* 24[1].
     This diphthong is written *aey* except in *blaeidaz* 90[4]
     (cf. *blaeyddiz* 81[7] and *blaeyde/i* 83[8], 89[2].

3)   ` *aey* by *R*-umlaut: c. g. *aeyro* 6[14].

4)   *á*: Forms of *hár* c. g. 44[11], cf. Ark., I, 266; forms
     of *fár* 42[10], 81[8].

5)   ⟩ *ó* ` *o*, originally in syllables with secondary accent:
     brott (adv.) 27 t. c. g. 43[8], 98[13] (cf. forms with *au*
     6 t. c. g. 21[6], 60[1]).

§ 14. Germanic *eu*

1)   *io* (before *a. o*),   *ió*: c. g. *briota* 78[5], *kiosa* 41[13],
     forms of *þiofr*, c. g. 62[4].

2)   *iu* (before *i. u.*), ` *iú*: c. g. *siukr* 81[6], 82[1]. This *iú* `
     ý by *i*-umlaut: c. g. *hýdr* 85[13] (*bjoda*), *kyss* 93[3]
     (*kiosa*).

CHAPTER II.

VOWELS IN SYLLABLES WITH SECONDARY ACCENT OR
UNACCENTED.

A. Variation of *e/i*.

§ 15. In Noreen, Gr., § 124, 2, Hom. Ll., p. 88; Sievers,
Tüb. Br., p. 11, rules are given, according to which the use
of these vowels is regulated in Norwegian dialects. All these
rules agree essentially, as the same principle prevails, that is,
that *e* is used after the less palatal vowels *a*, *e*, *o* and *i* after
the *i*- and *u*-vowels.

These vowels in El. are not used in accordance with
this principle, although there are traces of the existence in a
former period of such a law.

After the vowels where we might expect *e*, in accordance
with the principle just stated, namely *a*, *e*, *o*, *ae*, *oe*, we find
the vowels distributed as follows: after *a* 360 t. *i* ∼ 273 *e*;
after *e*, 470 *i* ∼ 39 *e*; after *o*, 175 *i* ∼ 10 *e*; after *ae* 175
i ∼ 27 *e*; after *oe* 43 *i* ∼ 4 *e*.

The vowels after which we expect *i* are *i*, *u*, *y*, *au*
(diph.). We find after *i*, 352 *i* ∼ 94 *e*; after *u* 118 *e*   9 *e*;
after *y* 74 *i* ∼ 25 *e*; after *au* 15 *i* ∼ one *e*.

Clearly the so-called vowel-harmony does not exist here, yet, since the proportion of *e*'s is greater in the cases where it might be expected, it is evident that such a law did at one time exist, but that the dialect is at this time in a transition period tending toward a uniform use of *i*, as in the later Icelandic mss.

The total number of *i*'s is 2350, of *e*'s 575. Of these 575 cases where *e* is retained, 51 belong to the forms of one word, *sidderi*, but this is the only case where a single word or single category seems to have been instrumental in preserving the *e*. In certain dialects it seems that some entirely different principle regulated the use of *e/i*, that certain words or categories had one vowel or the other independently of the preceding vowel. An examination of the ms., with a view to establishing such a principle, results as follows: In the forms of the suffixed article *i* occurs 205 times, *e* 8 times. Suffix -*leg* -*lig*, *i* 78 t. ~ *e* 48 t., *ae* 2 t. Usually, in this suffix the vowel varies in the same word, *e. g. virdnligr* 4 t. ~ -*leg* 3 t., *dyrligr* 13 t. ~ -*leg* 8 t. Suffix -*ing* -*eng*: -*ing* 138 t. *eng* twice. Pres. ppl. -*ande'*-*andi*: *ande* 30 t. ~ -*andi* 4 t. *e. g. farande* 35[3], 43[9], *komande* 99[5] ~ -*andi* 90[14]. 111[6]. Pret. ppl. -*inn!*-*it*: *i* prevails here, *e* being used but once or twice, *e. g. fallinn* 11[6] etc., *dragit* 24[8].

In the above word-formative suffixes there certainly is a preference for one vowel, but it is the vowel *i* which is, as we have seen, the prevailing vowel throughout.

In the inflectional suffixes the vowels are more equally distributed, *e. g.* in the 3rd sg. pret. a very large category – they are nearly equal; *audvarpade* 3 t. *e. g.* 15[6] ~ -*di* 2 t. *e. g.* 85[1], *hafde* 21 t. *e. g.* 42[14] ~ -*di* 22 t. *e. g.* 26[6]. In the dat. sg. m. n.: *e* 70 t. ~ *i* 41 t. *e. g. lande* 11 t. *e. g.* 93[10], *snerde* 8 t. *e. g.* 11[5] ~ -*di* 15 t. *e. g.* 110[1]; n. pl. m.: *e* 17 t. ~ *i* 22 t. *e. g. badir* 8 t. *e. g.* 77[8] ~ *bader* 29[14], *hinir* 11 t. ~ -*er* once. A few adverbs keep one or the other vowel quite consistently: *alldri* 5 t. *e. g.* 71[12] ~ *alldre* 26 t. *e. g.* 12[3], *alldrigi* 107[12] ~ *alldregi* 25 t. *e. g.* 64[8], *alldrege* 39[8] ~ *alldre igi* 25 t. *e. g.* 1[9].

The above examples do not furnish sufficient evidence for a law regulating the vowels according to suffixes, and it is better to conclude, as was stated above, that the usual Nor-

wegian vowel-harmony once prevailed, but that the dialect is
now in a transition period, tending toward the use of *i* uniformly,
as in Icelandic.

B. Variation of *u/o*.

§ 16. There is no greater regularity in the use of these
vowels than in the use of *i e*.

The statistics are as follows: After the following vowels
where *o* is regular, according to the rule for Norwegian (cf. refe-
rences given above for *i e*), we find: after *e*, 108 *u* ~ 76 *o*,
after *o*, 102 *u* ~ 46 *o*, after *oe*, 12 *u* ~ 42 *o* after *ǫ*, 207
u ~ 201 *o* (*honom* 128), after *ae* 44 *u* ~ 7 *o*, after *ú*, 36
u ~ 44 *o*.   After the vowels where *u* is regular we find:
after *ǚ* 11 *u* ~ 3 *o*, after *i* 474 *u* ~ 19 *o*, after *u* 64 *u*
~ 2 *o*, after *y* 47 *u* ~ 17 *o*, after *aei* 30 *u* ~ 3 *o*. The
total number of *u*'s is 874 ~ 457 *o* (128 *honom*). Here too
it is evident that *u* preponderates, as *i* does, though the
proportion is not so large. It is also evident that *u* preponderates in the very cases where *o* would be regular, which
points, as in the case of *i/e*, to the former existence of a law
of vowel-harmony.

It is quite as impossible to arrange these forms in categories with special endings as in the case of *i/e*. If we might
expect uniformity in any form it would be in the ending *-um*
(cf. Hom., Ll. p. 94), yet we find here *-um* 433 t. ~ *-om*
247 t. (128 of these belong to *honom* and may be due to some
special reason). The only large categories where *u/o* occurs
with any sort of regularity are the above mentioned *honum*
which has *-um* 7 t. ~ *-om* 128 t. c. g. *-um* 98[6], 98[8] ~ *-om*
31[14], 33[4]; forms of *varr* (poss.): *varo* 7[3], 61[18], *varom* 8 t.
c. g. 82[4], forms of *veru*: *varo* 11 t. c. g. 36[13] ~ *voro* 22 t.
c.g. 104[6]. Aside from these words, complete irregularity prevails;
c. g. *drapu* 40[12] ~ *drapo* 18[6], 70[7], *radum* 1[10], 4[9] ~ *radom*
73[8], *acinum* 22[10] ~ *acinom* 88[9], *bryniu* 14 t. c. g. 6[13] ~
brynio 5 t. c. g. 5[12].

In the oldest part of Hom. *e* and *o* are regular without
regard to the preceding vowel, in the younger parts there is
a well regulated vowel-harmony. Cf. Hom., Ll. pp. 93, 94.
The ms. of El. is later still, having passed through the stage of
vowel-harmony and adopted the later Icelandic rule of *i* and *u*.

C. Other vowel changes.

§ 17. Suffix -*ari* -*eri*. Forms with and without umlaut occur, the variation being due originally to a difference in accent; *e. g. falseri* 85¹², 105⁸ ∾ *scapare* 15³, *ridderi* 15 t. *e. g.* 96¹ ∾ -*arile* 5 t. *e. g.* 44¹⁵. The variation of vowel appears also, through leveling, in forms where no *i* followed; *e. g. ridderar* 9 t. *e. g.* 22², *ridderum* 43¹² ∾ *riddaro(m)* 10¹³. *ridderascap* 1² ∾ *riddarascap* 6⁶.

§ 18. Suffix -*andi endi*. Umlauted forms of this suffix appear in *rangendo(m)* 1¹¹, forms of *tidendi* 5 t. *e. g.* 73⁹.

§ 19. Germanic *ō* in unaccented syllables.

According to Noreen, Gr., § 117, a. 2, Germanic *o* appears finally as *a*, in Norwegian quite regularly, having crowded out the regular *o* (bef. *u o*) throughout the paradigm. This is not regularly the case in El. but the following instances occur: *hrgnastu* 78¹⁶, *rikastu* 30⁷ ∾ *rikustu* 22², *skiotaztu* 92³, *samblandadum* 2⁷ ∾ *biorblandodu* 61¹, *skun(n)dadum* 18³, *stiornadu* 1⁶.

§ 20. *y* is umlauted to *i* before *i* of the following syllable, cf. Noreen, Gr., § 126. The following examples occur: *ivir* 5⁴ ∾ *yfir* 9 t. *e. g.* 86¹¹, *yfer* 3 t. *e. g.* 7¹⁴, *firer/ir* 82 t. *e. g.* 104³ ∾ *fyrir* 68⁵, 92¹⁴, *iunifli* 46² ∾ *innyfli* 38¹, 61², *hibyli* 88¹⁵, *hibylum* 8¹³. 14⁸.

§ 21. Miscellaneous.

1) Contraction does not appear, where we should expect it, in *ddir* 2¹, *seet* 10⁸ (ppl. of *sid*).

2) *a* is elided in *gef ee* 63⁶.

3) The form of the 3ʳᵈ pl. is used for the 3ʳᵈ sg. in *soekia* 82⁷.

CHAPTER III.

ACCENT.

§ 22. Where the acute accent is used, it marks a long vowel, usually, and corresponds to the Icelandic accent. In the majority of cases however the quantity of the vowels is left unmarked. The accent is used as follows:

1) over *a* 67 times; *e. g. á* (prep. and adv.) 23 t. ∾ *a* m. t., *á* (fem. subst.) 41¹, *ddir* 2¹ (here the accent on the second vowel indicates that the two are to be

kept apart:, $\acute{a}$ (. $eiga$) 5 t. $\sim$· a 6 t., $\acute{a}t$ (. eta 60[8],
61[8]), $f\acute{a}$ 60[7] $\sim$· fa 9 t. $e.$ $g.$ 78[12], $h\acute{a}lsi$ 42[7] $\sim$·
forms of $hals$ 11 t. $e.$ $g.$ 30[4], $l\acute{a}gt$ (adv.) 11[8] $\sim$ $lagt$
95[11], $s\acute{a}to$ 21[13] $\sim$ $satu$ 86[11], forms of $varr$ (poss.)
with accent 5[14]. 20[8]. 28[8] $\sim$· forms without accent
27 t.

2) over e 12 times: $l\acute{e}t$ (. $lata$) 5 t. $e.$ $g.$ 17[13] $\sim$· let
   7 t. $e.$ $g.$ 13[4], $m\acute{e}r$ 14[5] $\sim$ mer 102 t.

3) over o 20 times: $b\acute{o}klaerdr$ 17[5] $\sim$ bok 3 t. $e.$ $g.$ 116[7],
   $d\acute{o}ma$ 10[2] $\sim$· $domu(m)$ 17[2], forms of $g\acute{o}dr$ 2 t. 102[8]
   (bis) $\sim$· forms of $godr$ 14 t., $\acute{o}n$ (prep.) 62[10], 74[11]
   $\sim$· on 62[4]. 79[2].

4) over io 3 times: $e.$ $g.$ $li\acute{o}p$ 66[4], 102[2] $\sim$· $liop$ 17 t.,
   $ti\acute{o}n$ 77[10].

5) over u 12 times: $e.$ $g.$ $h\acute{u}s$ 109[4], $\acute{u}t$ 5 t. $e.$ $g.$ 99[16] $\sim$
   ut m. t., $\acute{u}mb\acute{o}t$ 3[6], (may be dittography here).

6) over y 2 times: — $f\acute{y}st$ 61[4], $on\acute{y}t$ 101[9] $\sim$ forms of
   $onyttr$ $nyttr$ 6[10], 6[8].

7) over au 13 times: — 8 t. over second vowel, 5
   times over first — $e.$ $g.$ $bra\acute{u}t$ 21[6] bis, 21[10] $\sim$·
   $brautt$ 87[7], $braut$ 15[6], $br\acute{a}ut$ 60[1], $l\acute{a}uf$ 45[2] $\sim$ $lauf$
   in compounds and derivatives 7 t., $la\acute{u}fgullta$, $sca\acute{u}t$
   101[7] $\sim$ $skaut$ 7 t. There seems to be no reason
   for placing the accent over one vowel rather than
   the other, since the same word occurs with the
   accent in both positions, cf. above — $bra\acute{u}t$ — $l\acute{a}uf$.

8) over ae 60 times: $e.$ $g.$ $ga\acute{e}fa$ 26[11] $\sim$ $gaefa$ 3 t.
   $e.$ $g.$ 79[6], $ha\acute{e}tta$ 114[6] $\sim$· $haetta$ 3 t. $e.$ $g.$ 13[4], $ma\acute{e}r$
   6 t. $\sim$ $maer$ 18 t.

9) over aei once — $\not{p}\acute{a}eir$ 43[7] $\sim$ $\not{p}aeir$ m. t.

10) over ϱ once -- $f\acute{\varrho}rt$ 60[14].

General remarks on Vocalism.

The manuscript betrays marked Icelandic characteristics in
several important points, namely, the younger u-umlaut of a
and $\acute{a}$; the falling together in sound of ϱ and $\acute{a}$; the prevailing
use of i in unaccented syllables. This fact, together with the
absence of any decided East Norse characteristics, marks the
dialect as being West Norwegian.

PART II.

CONSONANTS.

CHAPTER IV.

GERMANIC CONSONANTS.

§ 23. Germanic *p*

1) = *p*:—a) When medial; *c. g. apalldrs* 66[5], forms of *drepa, c. g.* 19[6].

 b) When final; *gracip* 5 t. *c. g.* 98[9], forms of *skip, c. g.* 20[5].

 c) In combination with *s* — *c. g. sprungu* 106[2], *spotti* 12[12], forms of *spiot, c. g.* 5[13].

2) *f* in the combination *pt*. This is a peculiarity of Norwegian dialects and is somewhat rare. Cf. Noreen, Gr., § 191. The following instances occur in El.: *lacyfti* 6 t. *c. g.* 25[13] ∽ *lacypti n* 6 t. *c. g.* 13[6], *stacyftiz* 33[4] ∽ *stacyptiz* 66[7], -*n* 40[11]. The combination *pt* occurs in *snacyptr* 100[4], *ocpti c n* 12 t. *c. g.* 100 [12], *kipti* 64[1].

3) *pp* — originally when final, thence by transfer to medial position, *c. g. upp* 32 t. *c. g.* 106[14], *uppi* 89[1]. 114[1].

 All words with initial *p* are loan-words. Examples of these are *paradisi* 76[2], *pascu(m)* 4[7], *pellz* 73[13].

§ 24. Germanic *pp*

1) = *pp, c. g. slyppr* 66[1].

2) *p* before another consonant; *c.g. kipti* 64[1] (⟨ *kippa*), *kapsamliga* 44[15] (*mp* cf. *m* p. 28).

§ 25. Germanic *b*

1) = *b* — occurs only after nasals: — forms of *dramb, c. g.* 50[13].

 Words with initial *b* (if not from *b* are loan-words, *c. g. bellti* 87[2], *braczi* 78[6].

2) Assimilations: — *mb* *mm* in syllables with weak accent, and is further simplified to *m, c. g. um* (prep.) m. t. *c. g.* 3[1].

3) *b* is lost in *dramsama* 37[4] ∽ forms of *dramb* m. t.

§ 26. Germanic *b*

1) = *b* initially, *c. g. buna* 106[4], forms of *barn* 9 t.
c. g. 23[7].

2) > *f* (a voiced dento-labial spirant); *c. g. arf* 4[14],
forms of *dracifa, c. g.* 112[9], *klifa* 40[5], *lof* 30[16], *lacifa*
61[2], *ofan* 9 t. *c. g.* 60[10].

This sound is represented by *v* in the following
words: 53 t. *gevi* 74[10] ∼ *gefi* 10 t. and many other
forms and derivatives, all written with *f*; the following
forms of *hava: hava* 22 t. *c. g.* 42[11] (*hana* 91[9]
∼ *hafa* 9 t. *c. g.* 18[10]), *hevi* 9 t. ∼ *hefi* 6 t.,
hevir 3[6], 64[11] ∼ *hefir* 50 t. *c. g.* 3[7], *havom, hovom*
4 t. (all other forms of *hava* have *f*); *hovod* 68[4] ∼
forms with *f* 27 t. and *haufdingi* 15 t.; *liva* 3 t. *c. g.*
8[5] ∼ *lifa* 9[13], *livande/a* 3 t. *c. g.* 36[1] (∼ *lifande*
4 t. *c. g.* 81[1]), *livi* 1[6], 7[3] ∼ *lifi* 12[8], 30[11], *olivis*
74[13] ∼ *olifis* 112[5] (other forms with *f*); *sialvum om*
3 t. *c. g.* 25[10] ∼ *sialfum, siolfum* 4 t. *c. g.* 75[13] (in
all other forms, *f*); *ivir* 5[4] — *yfir* 12 t. *c. g.* 113[4];
athacvi 42[1].

3) *fn* > *mn* (This is the *f* of § 27. 2.). This is a
Norwegian development and occurs under different
conditions in different dialects. Cf. Noreen, Gr.,
§ 182. 2 and Hom. Ll., p. 108.

The cases where this occurs, or might be expected,
in El. are as follows: *iamnan* (adv.) 1[11], 76[3] ∼
iafnan 5 t., *iamningi* 45[12] ∼ *iafn(n)ingar* 9[8], *iam-*
in cpds. 12 t. (followed by *f, g, m, v*), *iafnligast*
27[10], *athofn* 40[10], *hemna* 39[11] ∼ *hefna* 17[2], 102[5]
(*fn* in other forms of this word, 3 t. before a
vowel, 2 t. before *d* and *t*), *snefn* 96[9], *suefnloft*
73[10], 75[4]. This is rather scanty material on which
to set up a rule, but the tendency seems to be,
fn > *mn* in a syllable with weak accent, *c. g. iam-*
15 t. (cf. Hom. Ll., p. 109, foot-note) ∼ *iafn* once,
and this change may occur before a vowel; *c. g. mn*
in the above list 4 t. ∼ *fn* 13 t. (cf. p. 28).

One instance occurs of *f* > *m* before a nasal vowel,
helmingr 84[6].

4) *f* (unvoiced) before *k* and *s*; *c. g. alfkonur* 65⁶, 86⁹, (cf. Kluge, s. Alp.), *þrjskn* 65².

§ 27. Germanic *f* (unvoiced)

1) = *f*, when initial; forms of *fara*, *c. g.* 8², 9¹⁴, *fotr*, *c. g.* 95¹⁰.

2) *f* (voiceless dento-labial spirant), after a vowel or *l, r*, except when *k, s*, or *t* follows: forms of *afl, c. g.* 60⁹, *hofa* 92⁸, *ocfra* 14⁶, forms of *akafr* 6 t. *c. g.* 12⁷ ∼ *akavom* 5³. This latter is the only instance where *v* is written for this sound.

3) ⟩ *þ* before *s, t*. There is no apparent rule for this change, cf. Noreen, Gr., § 185, 2, Hom. Ll., p. 109.
The cases are *acpt*(*cr*) 41⁴ (∼ *ft* 16 t.), *giptid* 88¹² (∼ *giftid* 81² and other forms with *ft* 9 t.), *lopt* 90³ (∼ *ft* 4 t.), forms of *lrpt* 44¹⁴, 13⁴, 97² (∼ *ft* 22¹⁰, 97⁸), *optasamliga* 21⁴ (∼ *oft* 64¹², 71⁹), *optarr* 42⁸, 39⁶ (∼ *oftarr/r* 42², 65¹, 8¹³), *spiotscapt* 21⁹, 26⁶ (∼ *ft* 35¹⁵, 35¹⁶), *vidrscipti'c* 29¹¹, 104⁴. Other words where only *ft* appears are: forms of *kraftr* 3 t. *c. g.* 31², forms of *kroftugr* 72⁷, 75¹⁰, *refsingum* 94⁷, forms of *skifta* 3 t. *c. g.* 27¹⁰, *aftr* 10 t *c. g.* 102¹³.
The above examples show that this tendency is not well established in El. for there are only 13 ex. of *pt* and in every case, except *vidrscipti*, the same word has a greater number of forms with *ft*.

4) *f* is lost in *fim* 21¹², 62¹⁰, *fimtu* 44¹⁰. In *fimtu f* is dropped because it is in a group of three consonants. *fim* follows the analogy of the ordinal.

§ 28. Germanic *t*

1) = *t*; forms of *taka, c. g.* 14¹⁵, 67⁸, *tima* 25¹⁰, forms of *fotr, c. g.* 95¹⁰.

2) ⟩ *d* when final, unaccented, and preceded by a vowel, 7 times; *brotid* (ppl.) 26⁶ (∼ *brotit* 63¹⁰), *getid* (ppl.) 95¹, *latid* (ppl.) 66¹¹, 100⁴, 106¹⁴. In these participial forms the *d* (= *t*) is from *tt* *nt*.
d is used also in the forms of the suffixed article twice; *briostid* 75¹², *loptid* 90³ ∼ *t* many times.

2*

In all of the above cases the syllable begins with *t*. This seems to indicate a tendency to such a dissimilation as exists in certain Icelandic mss., cf. Noreen, Gr., § 192. The dissimilation is not completely carried out, however, for *t* occurs in *briostit* 33[3], *spiotit* 35[14].

3) *tt* after a long vowel with chief stress:

When originally final; *c. g. brott* (adv.) 27 t. *c. g.* 7[6], 12[8] ∼ *brot* 5 t. *c. g.* 42[9], *dyrtt* (adj.) 44[1], 62[8] ∼ *dyrt* 5 t. *c. g.* 11[10], *crtt* (⟨ *vera*) 83[6] ∼ *crt* 30 t. *c. g.* 115[7] (The single occurrence of this word, which is usually unaccented, with *tt* is probably due to careless writing), *boettr* 35[2], *satt* (2 sg. pt. ⟨ *sia*) 34[12], 23[12] (with acct.), *fatt* 81[7].

In *gaetti* 32[14] the reason for doubling is not clear, (cf. *giaeta* 107[9]). Cf. Ark., V, 121 f. In *boettr* we have an example of sporadic lengthening of *t* before *r*, cf. Noreen, Gr., § 220 a. 2.

4) *tt* stands for Latin *t* in forms of *natturuligr* 3 t. *c. g.* 24[10] ∼ *t* 1[8].

5) *tk* is assimilated to *kk*; *c. g.* forms of *nockor* with *ck* 15 t. ∼ *cc* 33[14].

6) a) *t* + *s* is written *z* with the value of *ts* in *bliaz* 73[12], *skatz* 78[14].

b) *t* is dropped in the following cases: *fai* (*per* follows) 63[11]; *hinga* 70[2] (∼ *hingat* 11 t. *c. g.* 24[2]. The dropping of *t* in *hingat* is undoubtedly due to careless writing. D has *hingat* and D is based on the same original, but as it is much later and greatly changed, it proves nothing as to the form of the word in the original.

§ 29. Germanic *tt*

= *tt*, *c. g. hetti* 43[2], forms of *skattr* 4 t. *c. g.* 79[2].

§ 30. Germanic *d*

1) = *d* (occurs only after nasals); forms of *binda*, *c. g.* 6[1], 10[12], forms of *hond*, *c. g.* 30[14], *undir er* 13 t. (∼ *undir* 69[7]).

2) *t:* a) when final after *n; e. g. batt* 98[15], 101[4].

b) when final after *l; e. g. giallt* 62[7], *gallt* 11 t",
hellt (*hallda*) 9 t. *c. g.* 36[5].

c) before *s* (written *z*) in *lan(n)z* 20[3].

3) *d(d)t*) *tt; e. g. foctt* 3[6], 65[6].

4) *d* is lost in a group of three consonants; *an(n)suor*
45[10], *vauligast* 64[14], *brugnu* 113[13].

§ 31. Germanic *d*

1))*d:* — a) when initial; forms of *dottir, e. g.* 78[18], *disca* 61[11].

b) after *l, m, n,* regularly, but the following words
have some forms with *d: fioldi* 4 t. *c. g.* 116[1]
(cf. *fiolde* 40[7]), *skilde/i* 6 t. *c. g.* 45[10], *skilldumz*
18[5] (~ *skilde* 24[12], 36[9], (*ll*) 38[14], *vesoldum*
38[2] (~ *vesallda* 37[7], *-der* 3 t. *c. g.* 16[7], *samde*
4[7] (cf. *samde* 86[9]), *socmd* 3[11], *-dar* 8[11] (cf.
socmd 6 t. *-dar a* 4 t.), *-scmd* 10[4], *-ar* 12[11] (cf.
-scmd 4 t. *c. g.* 10[3], *-ar* 19[5]).

The change of *d* to *d* in this position took
place in Norwegian, at about the time that this
ms. originated, occurring latest of all after a
short vowel. These words are remnants of
the older state. The last five words, it will be
noticed, have a short vowel. Cf. Hom. Ll.,
p. 106.

c) after *lg, ng.* Cf. Noreen, Gr., § 183, 1. b.

Two instances of this change occur; *frlgdar*
8[4], 5[7] (~ *-dar* 6[7], 107[3], 73[11] and other forms
with *lgd* 11 t.), *he(n)gde* 26[9] ~ *hengdr* 65[2].

2) = *d; c. g. bacid* 42[2], 66[1], *acyda* 61[11], forms of *hardr,*
c. g. 14[4], forms of *fadir c. g.* 71[10]. It is written *d* three
times, namely, *daudan* 25[7] (cf. *daudan* 31[10] and other
forms with *d* 20 t.), *gode* 62[1] (cf. *gode i* 4 t. *c. g.* 43[15]
and other forms with *d* 10 t.), *modir* 9[2] (cf. *modir* 05[3].

3) *t:* — a) after *s, c. g. kysti* 76[14], 102[1], *vaciztu* 69[10];

b) after *l* and *n* which are, or were once, preceded
by a voiceless consonant; *maellt* m. t. *c. g.*
26[14], *racnti* 94[10].

c) after *p* and *t, c. g. kipti* 64[1], *kacyfti* 24[1], *lacypti*
6 t. *c. g.* 13[6] (*ft* 6 t. *c. g.* 25[13]).

d) before *s*; *c. g. borz* 77[12]; but *dauds* 108[12], *guds* 8 t. *c. g.* 31[2]. In these forms *d* is retained through association. Further examples are the 2. pl. reflex. *buiz* 85[13], *kugiz* 88[9], *raediz* 88[9].

e) When final after a vowel with weak accent. *hundrat* 9 t. *c. g.* 62[6], *met* (prep.) 12 t. *c. g.* 7[10], 8[7] (cf. *med* 97 t. *c. g.* 67[9]), *vit* (prep.) 17[7], 69[15], 115[10] (cf. *vid* m. t., *uid* 88[1]), *haufut* 45[3] (cf. *-ud* m. t., *-up* 95[9], *ud* 110[9]). This last form may be explained as a transfer from the genitive, where *d ⟩ t* before *s*. Cf. Noreen, Gr., § 183. a. 10.

In a few cases *t* occurs in the 2 pl. of the verb; *nemit* 12[14], *latet* 7[4] (cf. *latid* 8[8], 42[9]), *takit* 62[9], *set* (⟨ *sia*) 4 t. *c. g.* 2[13] (cf. *sed* 5[8]).

This change occurs only dialectically and late in Icelandic (cf. Noreen, Gr. § 183. 2. f.). The verb forms, 2 pl., are explained as reduced from a double consonant arising from an enclitic. *dt ⟩ tt ⟩ t.* cf. Noreen, Gr., § 135, a. 1. The two words given above with *d*, namely, *vid* and *haufud* have *d* probably because the stroke in *d* was omitted. In *haufup* 95[9] we have the only instance of *p* final. It is probably dittography as *p* in *pegar* stands almost directly above it in the ms.

4) *d + d ⟩ dd, c. g. baciddiz* 44[3], 84[7], *blaeyddiz* 81[7], *foedde* 70[4].

5) Assimilations.

   a) Regressive.

      α. *dt ⟩ tt, c. g. klacitt* 109[13], *roett* 8[16], *gott* 5 t. *c. g.* 93[9].

      β. *dd ⟩ dd, c. g. aeydd* 101[9].

      γ. *dl ⟩ ll, c. g. millom* 4 t. *c. g.* 46[1], *milli* 66[5], 87[4].

   b. Progressive.

      α. *td ⟩ tt, c. g. gaettu* 97[7], pt. of *moeta* 5 t. *c. g. moetti* 113[5], *setti* 98[6], *-u* 21[4] (⟨ *setia*), *vardvacitti* 26[5].

      β. *Rd ⟩ dd;* forms of *rodd, c. g.* 29[1].

6) *d* is lost in a group of three consonants; *noerrœnu* 116[8], forms of *scurgud* 4 t. *e. g.* 107[12].

§ 32. Germanic *þ*

1) — *þ* when initial; *e. g. þiggia* 2[8], 22[10], forms of *þora, e. g. þorir* 23[4], *þackade* 43[6], 91[15].

2) *d*

a) after vowels; *e. g. knad* 70[3]. This *d* *t* before *s* and *ts* is written *z, e. g. abraeizl* 75[7].

b) after *r*; forms of *verda, e. g.* 9[7].

c) when initial in a syllable with weak accent, *e. g. kvidar* 33[11], forms of *klaedi, e. g.* 86[10], 86[11].

3) *f* in the combination *þl*, which begins a syllable; forms of *flvia, e. g.* 42[3], forms of *innrfli* 3 t. *e. g.* 33[4].

4) Assimilations.

a) *lþ* \ *ll, e. g.* forms of *allr* m. t. ∼ *l* once in *alt* 95[11], *all-* (pref.) 2 t. *e. g.* 80[14], 104[12], *al-* 5 t. *e. g.* 36[6], forms of *gull* 24 t. *e. g.* 87[2] (cf. *gnl-* 5[13]).

b) *uþ* *nn, e. g.* forms of *annarr* with *nn* m. t. (cf. *anarri* 111[10], *-a* 81[8]), forms of *skinn* 6 t. *e. g.* 38[11], forms of *nnna* 4 t. *e. g.* 76[8], forms of *finna, e. g.* 102[6].

5) is lost before *l*; forms of *mdl* 5 t. *e. g.* 23[7].

§ 33.

þþ a) *tt, e. g. spotti* 12[17], *þetta* 28 t. *e. g.* 116[2]. Cf. Ark., IV., 97.

b) *þ* *d* after a vowel with weak accent; *eda* 31 t. *e. g.* 4[6], *medan* 8 t. *e. g.* 36[2].

§ 34. Germanic *k*

1) — *k: folk* 5 t. *e. g.* 38[4], forms of *knikr, e. g.* 92[8], *lokit* 12[6].

For the writing *k c* see below. It is written once *qu* in *quad* 92[16] (cf. *knad* 143 t.). In *kiendi* 100[8], 111[2] the palatal consonant is indicated by *ki* which is rare before a palatal vowel. Other forms of this word have *k; kend-* 7 t. and *kenna* 30[12]. In the following cases, where a palatal *k* has come, through syncope of a palatal vowel, to stand before a non-palatal vowel, *i* is inserted to show the palatal quality: *fatockium* 2[1], -*an* 8[11], *mioddreckin* 75[9], *licneskiur* 22[8], -*a* 75[5], -*om* 87[9], *rikium* 8[16] (cf. *rikum* 5 t. *c. g.* 9[7]), *rikia* 2[9] (~· *rican* 89[14] etc.). In *kirkiu* 3[5] the preceding palatal vowel produces palatalization of *k.* cf. Noreen, Gr., § 204.

2) *k* + *i* ⟩ *kk, c. g. reckiu* 6 t. *c. g.* 75[6].
k + *u* ⟩ *kk, c. g. nockuidr* 62[16].

3) = *kk* before *l, c. g. macklig* 85[9], in forms of *mikill, ck* 16 t. *c. g.* 71[14] (*kk* in *mik-kla* 113[10]). In *styrck* 63[7] the reason for the gemination is not apparent.

§ 35. Germanic *kk*

= *kk, c. g. lokkari* 102[11], *loccat* 37[4], *lockum* 1[5], forms of *flockr* 6 t. *c. g.* 41[14] (cf. *floks* 33[10]).

k/c — Both *k* and *c* are used to represent the voiceless guttural stop, but neither letter is used to represent exclusively either the palatal or the guttural, as is the case in many Norwegian mss. (In the following, all Norse *k*'s of whatever origin are included).

The single palatal voiceless explosive occurs about 430 times; of these only 11 are *c*'s: *cocmit* 63[8], *micit* 20[4], *scip* 22[9], *sciolldu* 10[19], *scialld-* 10[9], *scyli* 9[10], *vidrscipte* 104[4], *scylld* 4 t. Of these eleven, nine occur in the combination *sc.* This combination occurs as *sk* 162 times. Palatal geminata occurs 36 times, always *ck.* It appears from the above that *k* is the regular representative of palatal *k.*

The guttural voiceless explosive occurs about 1335 times. Of these, 594 are *c*'s (including *cc* 225 t.). *c* (guttural) occurs initially, medially and finally, especially in combination with *s: sk* 66 times ~· *sc* 168 times; *taka* 4 t. *c. g.* 67[8] ~· *taca* 7 t. *c. g.* 73[8], *miok* 3 t. *c. g.* 97[1], ~ *mioc* 23 t. *c. g.* 87[12], *kaullodu* 20[12], ~ *calladi* 10[9]. *k* occurs as initial more frequently than *c.* Guttural geminata occurs 80 times; *ck* 73 t. ~ *kk* 5 t. ~ *cc* 2 t. *c. g. drecka* 33[12], 75[14]. Four out of the five *kk*'s occur where the word is divided at the end of the line, *c. g. lok--kari* 102[11]. The two instances of *cc* are *loccat* 37 , *noccorrom* 33[14]. The combination *cl* occurs chiefly in two words *claedi* and *mikill.* In forms of *claedi, kl* occurs 19 t. ~ *cl* 25 t. In forms of *mikill, kl* 3 t. ~ *cl* 31 t. When final before *t,* the

stop which comes from *g* occurs 15 t. always as *c*, *e. g. faegilæt*
3[4]. In six cases final *k* (which has been included among the
gutturals), is followed by the palatal vowel of the suffixed article.
In these cases it is always written *k*.

The above figures show that *k* is used in the majority
of cases for both palatal and guttural. The geminata is nearly
always *ck*, whether palatal or guttural.

§ 36. Germanic *g*

1) = *g*:

forms of *godr*, *c. g. godan* 89[1], forms of *gud*, *c. g.*
3[7], forms of *gefa*, *c. g.* 5[11], *lengr* (adv.) 5. t. *c. g.*
95[3], *mega* 114[12], *laúg* 76[10].

Before a non-palatal vowel *gi* is written, to indicate
a palatal *g*, in the following words: *haedingia* 32[9],
-iar 91[8], *aerfingia* 3[1], *fraegia* 76[4], 110[2], *giorst* 103[13],
giorsamliga 62[4], *giarkuelld* 99[12], *hoegiasto* 93[12], forms
of *eug* (pl.) 4 t. *c. g.* 34[3].

Once, in *giegnum* 60[11], *gi* represents palatal *g*.

2) *k*: – a) after *s*, *c. g. enskiz* 81[1].

b) after *t*, *c. g. huartki* 5 t. *c. g.* 7[6].

c) before *t*, suf. *-ect -ict*, *c. g. kunnict* 7 t. *c. g.*
69[10], *faegilect* 3[1].

d) before *h*; forms of *katr* (**ʒahahtaκ*) 3 t. *c. g.*
77[8].

3) *ng* final, *nk* ˅ *kk*, *c. g. feck* 36[3], 106[9] (~· *fek* 26[7],
98[2], 70[10] (*c*), *fect* 23[8]), *gack* 4 t. *c. g.* 38[1] (~· *gak*
38[10], 103[1]), *geek* 14 t. *c. g.* 114[13] (~· *gek* 97[7]),
heck 3 t. *c. g.* 87[4]. The forms with single consonant
are due to the fact that these verbs were often
unaccented in sentence combination, in which case
the simplification wonld be regular.

4) *g + i* *gg*: forms of *leggia*, *c. g.* 69[4], *tueggia* 115[10],
forms of *skegg*, *c. g.* 1˅, forms of *orugger* 4 t. (~· *g*
20[10], 114[12], simplified in a final consonant group).

5) *g + u* *gg*: Forms of *hogg* have *gg* 24 t. (~· *haugs*
3 t. *c. g.* 45[17]), forms of (*h*)*ryggia*, *ryggr* *-gg* 7 t.
(~· *ryglaeik* 71[11], cf. *rygglaeik* 21[14]). The forms
with single consonant are due to the regular dropping

of g where a group of three consonants arises. Where the double consonant appears, as in *rygglacik*, it is restored, or rather preserved, by association. — *tryggnan* 115[14], forms of *skuggi* 3 t. *c. g.* 60[11].

Of similar origin is probably the *gg* in *cnggarrar* 91[2] ($\langle$ *ong(v)arrar*).

b) is lost

in *lacyndiz* 68 Goth. (*ga-laugnjan*). Cf. also the loss of g noted above.

§ 37. Germanic h

1) $= h$ when initial before u, i (voiceless spirant), *c. g.* *huossum* 43[3], forms of *hvitr*, *c. g.* *huitu* 6[12].

2) — h (breathing) when initial before a vowel; forms of *hafa*, *c. g.* 21[13], forms of *hundr*, *c. g.* 22[13].

3) voiceless l, n, r, before l, n, r, and is then lost; forms of (h) *lacia*, *c. g.* 74[1], forms of (h)*lutr*, 31[7], forms of (h) *raustr*, *c. g.*31[15].

There are only three instances in El. of the retention of h, namely, *hrid* 76[11], *hncfum* 61[15], *hliop* 31 (cf. *liop* m. t.). These are due to the influence of the Icelandic.

4) *hv* before *o* ` h, *c. g.* *horfa* 7[8], *hót* 92[1].

5) k after a short vowel before s;

forms of *vaxa*, *c. g.* 26[12], *fax* 95[10], *sextigir* 3[2], *vexi* 37[11], 73[3], *oxl.* 6 t. *c. g.* 29[3].

6) Assimilation. $ht \rangle tt$:

atti ($\langle$*ciga*) 3 t. *c. g.* 41[16], forms of *dottir* m. t. *c. g.* 69[13], forms of *drottin* m. t. *c. g.* 16[5] (cf. *drotni(n)g* 101[6]), *flaettingu(m)* 87[4] $\sim$ *t* 95[11], forms of *haetta* 4 t. *c. g.* 114[6], *haetti* ('*háttr*) 3 t. *c. g.* 82[6], forms of *mega*, *matt* etc. m. t. *c. g.* 31[2], forms of *nott*, *c. g.* 71[17] (cf. *nactr* 64[12], *natsonge* 12[6]), *ottumz* 92[13], *rettr* 81[13], forms of *slettr*, *c. g.* 92[3], *potti* 5 t. *c. g.* 11 , forms of *aett* 6 t. *c. g.* 6[9].

7) h is lost:

c. g. *á* 41[1], *dár* 2[1], *bra* (*bregda*) 4 t. *c. g.* 98[17], forms of *fa*, *c. g.* 5[6], forms of *licamr* 7 t. *c. g.* 12[4], *birtiz* 72[1], 87[9] (Ger. *bairhts*), *þusundrat* 78[2] ($\sim h$ 94[15]), *ins* 17[10] (= *hins*).

§ 38. Germanic *l*

1) - *l*, *c. g.* forms of *andlit* 16[17], 19[1], *blad* 66[8], *-lig* m. t.

2) voiceless *l* when initial, cf. examples under § 37, 3.

3) = *ll*

a) before *d*, *c. g. alldre* 1[7], *apalldrs* 66[5].

The ms. has regularly *ll* in this position. Only the following examples of *l* occur: *heldo* 112[9] (~ *helldo* 95[7], *-n* 70[11], 70[13]), *scattgildi* 80[1] (~ *-gilldr* 78[16]), *skilde* 24[12], 36[9], (*skilde* 5 t. *c. g.* 102[15], *skilldi* 38[14]), *landtialde* 93[5] (~ *landtialldi* 98[15], 112[6]), *vesoldnm* 38[2] (~ *vesalldr* 3 t. *-a* 37[7]), *dueldnmz* 14[10], *fiolde* 40[7] (*ld* 4 t. *c. g.* 36[12]).

The above cases of single *l* are due to the analogy of *ld* which does not regularly *lld* except in *hallda* 107[5] ~ *lld* 6 t.

b) before *t*, *c. g. bellti* 87[2], *follt* 17[7].

The only exceptions are *gult* 95[10], *maclti* 3 t. *c. g.* 13[2] (~ *ll* 62 t.), *scalt* 6 t. (~ *scallt* 30 t.), *skilt* 5 t. *c. g.* 19[2], *alt* 95[11] (~ *allt* m. t. *lt*). Single consonants are due, as above, to the analogy of *ld*.

c) The above cases of consonant lengthening are regular. Cf. Noreen, § 220, 3, 4. El. shows also the following cases of lengthening:

α) after *r*: *arlla* 28[5] (cf. *arla* 27[6], 112[12]), *ferllig* 32[10], *jarll* (a. s.) 114[9] (~ *iarls* 65[5], *-a* 21[3]), *jarlli* 76[5], *jorllnnn(m)* 42[11] (~ *l* 36[16]), *karlli* 88[18], *varlla* 29[9], 77[7], cf. Hom. Ll., p. 135, § 67, a. 2.

β) between vowels: *litilli* 70[11], *mikillar* 7[8], *-l* 7 t. *-a* 23[14]. All of these except the adverbs may be from the analogy of the nominative.

d) *l* is lost in *rekingi* 22[7], 44[5], 83[1] ~ *reklingr* 83[6].

§ 39. Germanic *ll*

= *ll*: forms of *fullr*, *c. g.* 44[6], *fella* 27[12], 36[14].

§ 40. Germanic *m*

1) - *m* in forms of *manadr*, *c. g.* 38[1], forms of *harmr*, *c. g.* 26[12].

2) *mn* *fn*, *c. g. nefndr*, 96[9], forms of *stefna* 4 t. *c. g.*
78[17], cf. § 26, 3.

3) Assimilations.

  a) *mp* > *pp*, in forms of *kapp*, 9 t. *c. g.* 82[6], 91[12],
(cf. *kapsamliga* 44[15]), forms of *stappa* 108[11], 75[13],
109[9].

  b) *mb* > *bb*, *c. g. klubbu* 66[5], 66[8], 67[12], cf. Noreen,
Gr., § 207, a, 4.

4) Loss of *m*.

  a) This occurs frequently before a pronoun com-
mencing with *v*.

    The following cases occur in El: *ero* (1st pl.),
followed by *vaer*, 20[4], 20[9], followed by *vit*, 34[2];
hongu, followed by *vit*, 77[8].

    vit (n. pl. du.) 115[10] is corrected by Ceder-
schiöld (cf. ref. in note, p. 2) to *mit*. If that
is the correct reading, we have here an illu-
stration of a peculiar assimilation, occurring only
in Norwegian dialects, of initial *v* of the pronoun
to final *m* of the preceding verb. The double
m, thus arising, is reduced to single *m*, so that
the verb is left without its final consonant, as in
this case, *skolu*.

  b) Other cases of the loss of *m* are: a) *fifl* 103[12],
before original voiceless *f*; b) when originally
final, *c. g. fra* (prep.) m. t. *c. g.* 110[1].

§ 41. Germanic *mm*

  = *mm*, *c. g. Grim(m)r* 11[9].

§ 42. Germanic *n*

1) = *n*, *c. g. nema* 7[1]. *ganga* 5[4].

2) / *nn*:

  a) before *d*, only in the following cases: 27 t.
annsuor c. g. 45[10], *bin(n)da* 6[1], 10[12] (~ *nd* m. t.),
ken(n)de 76[1] (cf. *nd* 8 t.), *lan(n)d* 74[11], *lan(n)z*
20[3] (~ *landz* 3 t.), *rin(n)da* 3 t. *c. g.* 27[4] (~ *nd*
m. t.), *sen(n)dom* 20[7], *sen(n)di* 78[9] (~ *nd* m. t.),
forms of *skunda* with *n(n)d* 26[9], 18[2], 71[2] (~ *nd*
m. t.), *u(n)ndan* 32[11] (~ *nd* 16 t.), *vau(n)de* 23[2],

62^{15}, -i 85^{12} ($\sim$ nd m. t.), forms of *hond* with
$n(n)d$ 5 t. ($\sim$ nd m. t.), forms of *hundr* with
$n(n)d$ 4 t. ($\sim$ nd m. t.).

Since these examples of *nnd* are comparatively
few, while *lld* is the rule, we may conclude that
in this dialect the doubling of *n*, which is just
beginning here, took place later than that of *l*.
In Hom. which, as we have seen, shows an older
stage in other respects, neither *l* nor *n* is doubled
regularly, cf. Hom. Ll., p. 134.

b) before *l*.

The instances of doubling are still fewer in this
case -- *renntir* 1^{10}, *ren(n)tir* 29^4 ($\sim$ *rent(er)*
86^1, *raentir* 94^3) are the only examples.

c) between vowels: *sin(n)a* (g. pl.) 5 t. c. g. 114^9
$\sim$ *sina* 1^5, *bacin(n)a* 2^1, which however is cor-
rected to *bacina* by Cederschiöld, (ref. above).

d) after *r*: α) before a vowel; *barn(n)a* 82^{10},
giarn(n)a (adv.) 8 t. c. g. 84^{12}, *girn(n)umz* 34^7,
-*iz* 81^2, *stiorn(n)ar* 110^{12} ($\sim$ *n* 105^{14}), *stiorn(n)adu*
1^6, *turn(n)i* 77^{10} ($\sim$ *turni* 72^{16}, 104^{11}), *turn(n)ar*
69^{11}, -*o* 71^8. β) final; *bor(n)n* 3^7, 38^8, *barn(n)*
62^9, *huern(n)* 8^6, 15^{15}, 61^{14}, *giarn(n)* 3 t. c. g.
11^9, *nockorn(n)* 89^7, 110^7, *stiorn(n)* 1^3, 82^{14},
turn(n) 115^{13} (cf. *turn* 3 t. c. g. 72^{11}), *rdarn(n)*
8^9, 63^2, (*r*) 15^{15}. γ) before *z*; *girn(n)zk* 99^4.

e) when final after a vowel as follows:
In the suffixed article, n. s. f., *in(n)* 59^{16}, a. s.
m. n., 66^5, 102^2, 110^6; pers. pron. *min(n)*, 96^4
($\sim$ *min* 7 t.); *mestan(n)* a. s. m. 41^{14}; *saman(n)*
4 t. c. g. 7^7, ($\sim$ *saman* 3 t. 16^2).

f) in other positions:
iafn(n)ingar 9^8, *mannz* 81^1 $\sim$ *manz* 61^{10}.

3) A single *n* occurs for double *n* in the following
forms of the suffixed article:
n. s. m. -*in* 96^{13}, 108^{10}, 115^1, d. s. f. -*ni* 113^5, a. s. m.
-*in* 66^5, 102^2, 110^6, — also in *hin* n. s. m. 24^{11}.
Some of these may be due to the omission of the
abbreviation for *n*.

4) Assimilations.
    a) *n* `m:—α*) before *þ*; *c. g. kompum* 41², (*au*) 22¹³.
           β) after *m* in *symmi* 33⁷, cf. Noreen, Gr.,
           § 252. 2.
    b) *n* ⟩ *t* before *d/t*;
        c. g. batt 98¹⁵, 101⁴, *acitt* 5 t. *c. g.* 8¹⁰, *mitt* 15 t.
        c. g. 93¹⁵, *satt* 24¹⁴, 62⁴, 105⁹, *sitt* 10 t. *c. g.* 13⁵,
        forms of *vetr* 6 t. *c. g.* 14⁸ (*tt* *t* in cons. group),
        þitt 4 t. *c. g.* 80⁴, (∼ *t* 83², 106⁹), forms of
        mottull 3 t. *c. g.* 86¹³ (cf. *motli* 73¹³).
5) *nnr* ⟩ *d*:
    In forms of *annarr*, *c. g. adrir* 65¹².
    In forms of *madr*, *c. g. madr* 4¹.
6) *n* is lost:
    a) Before *s*; *c. g.* forms of *ass* 12⁸, forms of *ast*,
        c. g. 59¹⁷, *musteri* 17¹³, forms of *fysa* 39¹².
    b) When originally final; *c. g.* á (prep.) m. t.

§ 43. Germanic *nn*

    = *nn*; *c. g. rann* 40¹², forms of *brenna*, *c. g.* 80⁴.

§ 44. Germanic *r*

1) = *r*; *c. g. brand* 61³, *giarn(n)a* 31¹⁵, *her* 3¹²,
    forms of *rikr*, *c. g.* 7⁸, *ord* 32¹⁰.
2) Initial voiceless *r* is written *hr* in *hrid* 76¹¹, other-
    wise *r*, *c. g. raustan* 1².
3) = *rr* in the following words:
    dyrrlega 28⁵, (*i*) 35⁵, 37², 77³ (∼ *r* m. t. *c. g.* 13¹¹);
    The *rr* is from analogy to the forms of the simple
    adj. where *rr* is regular, *c. g.* n. s. *dyrr.*
        optarr 39⁶, 42⁸, (*f*) 42², 65¹ (∼ *oftar* 8¹³); *fra-
marr* 90³.
        In these adverbs *rr* is transferred analogically from
adverbs like *naerr* where *rr* is regular, cf. Noreen,
Gr., § 221. 2. a. 2.
        In *hárr* 44¹¹, *sniorr* 73¹⁴, *rr* stands after the
analogy of many words which have *rr* regularly in
the nominative.
        ferr 81¹⁴ (1st sg.) is after the analogy of the
3rd sg. (cf. *fer* 1st sg. 28⁸, 71¹⁵). In *lend(r)ra* 2⁹,

where one *r* is an abbreviation, it may be due to careless writing.

4) *l* by dissimilation in *malmara* 2[6].

5) is lost in the following cases:

in *fosthrœdr* 16[1] (cons. group), *fyst* 62[9]. 97[9], *fystnnni* 11[13] (< *ss* *rs*), cf. Noreen, Gr., § 212. 3., *idulegar* 2[9], *fer* 98[13] (3. s.) transfer from 1st sg. ~ *ferr* (3. s.) 7 t.

In *fyr lata* 71[17] the syllable *ir* is lost (= *fyrir lata*).

§ 45. Germanic *rr*

= *rr* in *kyrr* 5[5], *fiarri* 28[15].

§ 46. Germanic *z* (urnord. *R*)

1) = *r*; e. g. *maer* 89[6], forms of *haeyra* 33[13], *dalr* 115[9], *sueri* 41[2].

2) Assimilations.

  a) Urgerm. *zl* , *ll?* in forms of *illr*, e. g. 14[13], cf. Noreen, Gr., § 208. a. 2.

  b) *Rd* > *dd*; *fon(n)* 87[5], forms of *rodd*, e. g. 29[1],

  c) *rR* > *rr*; e. g. *annarr* 20[1], *berr* 2[13], *fyrr* 21[10].

  d) *mR* ⸱ *mm* > *m* (with weak accent): *fram(m)* 8 t. e. g. 16[9] ~ *fram* 4 t. e. g. 101[15], *fra(m)mi* 34[2].

  e) *lR* > *ll*; e. g. *fetill* 115[1], *fioll* 92[2], forms of *iarll* 9 t. e. g. 15[8], (~ *iarl* 92[16]), *litill* 64[3].

  f) *nR* > *nn*; in *menn* m. t. e. g. 40[3], *fallinn* 97[2].

  g) *sR* ⸱ *ss*; e. g. *ass* 12[8], 13[8], *uiss* 77[8], *-lauss* 7 t. e. g. 39[8], (cf. *-lauS* 5[7]).

§ 47. Germanic *s*

1) = *s*, e. g. *sangu* 1[1], *lesa* 7[2], *disca* 61[11], *gras* 32[8].

2) *ss*:

hnerss 17[14], *hness* 31[4], *hnessu* 3 t. 110[14] (cf. *rss* 5 t. e. g. 12[15]). Possibly some of these are due to dittography, (Hom. Ll., p. 135).

3) is lost:

bernku 82[11] (cf. *sk* 98[11]), *hawerk lacik* 86[4] (cf. *sc* 1[8], *sk* 22[4]), *laetk* 81[6] (cf. *laezk* 82[1]).

§ 48. Germanic *ss*

= *ss*: *gassi* 23[4], *huossum* 43[4].

§ 49. Germanic *i*

1) = *i* (occurs only when medial after a short syllable), c. g. *bidia* 6[12].

2) Initial *i* occurs in the adv. *ia* and forms of *jungfru*, but these are loan-words.

This is written *j* twice in forms of *jungfru* 102[4], 85[4] (cap.) elsewhere *i*. The initial consonant which has developed in *ia* ⟨ *e* is written *j* in *Jarll* 41[1]. These are the only instances of the occurrence of *j* in the ms.

3) is lost when initial. Examples are forms of *ung*, c. g. 11[13].

§ 50. Germanic *u*

1) = *v*; a) when initial, c. g. *vita* 24[6].

    b) when medial, c. g. *ydvarn(n)* 15[15].

Both *u* and *v* are used to represent Germanic *u*. They are distributed as follows, when initial;

α) before *a* in forms of *uapnhest* 91[11], 93[12], 92[3] ~ forms of *vapn* m. t.;

β) before *e* in *uestan* 86[8] (~ *vestan* 74[9]), *ueria* (inf.) 103[13] (cf. *veria* 8 t.), *skipueria* 94[4];

γ) before *i* in *uid* (prep.) 18 t. *uid* 88[1] (~ *vid* m. t.), *uidi* 45[2] (cf. *vidr* 8 t.), *uidrskipti* 29[11] (~ *vidscipte* 104[4]), *uida* 69[1] (cf. *vida* 5[14], -*um* 73[12]), *uilldi* 109[10], 112[7], 110[12], *uil* 4 t. c. g. 101[1], *uilit* 84[13], 88[10], -*i* 99[8], *uilia* 91[9] (cf. forms of *vilia* m. t.), *uilldra* 101[5] (cf. forms of *villdr* 4 t.), *uili* 86[2], 90[1] (cf. *vilia* 75[5]), forms of *acinuigi* 3 t. (~ *v* 6 t.), *uinr* 95[12] (cf. forms of *vinr* m. t.), *uirdulegs* 1[2], *uirduliga* 19[8] (cf. forms of *virduligr* m. t.), *uirdingum* 90[2] (cf. forms of *virding* m. t.), *uirkdum* 86[4], *uiss* 77[8], -*u* 77[7], 92[14] (cf. forms of *viss* 5 t.), *uit* (pron.) 91[5], 115[10] (m.?) (cf. *vit* 9 t.), *uiti* 3[13] (cf. forms of *vit* 71[9], 77[7], 15[11] (vb.), forms of *heluiti* 19[6], 25[17], *uissi* 103[13], 108[1] (cf. *vissi* 110[13] and forms of *vita* m. t.).

δ) **before** *ae* in *naer* 90[7] (∼, *vaer* m. t.).

When not initial, *u* is regular, but *v* occurs in forms of *bolva* 11 t. *e.g.* *bolvade* 24[15] (cf. *bolui* 34[10]), -*svaem(n)* 16[6] (∼ forms of *suacinu* 9 t.), *Sī'a* 41[2] (cf. *sua* m. t.), *rdvaru(n)* 15[15].

2) is lost:

   a) before *u* and *o*;
   e.g. forms of *undra* 4[5], forms of *ord*, *c.g.* 100[16], *orti* 23[3], *ofin(u)* 86[12], (*t*) 86[12], (cf. *v* restored in -*vofuu* 5[13], -*n(m)* 73[12] bis), *höt* 92[1].

   b) before *l*; *c.g.* *andlit* 16[12], 19[1].

   c) when final, in *kné* 64[3], 65[3].

   d) analogically in *kefia* 83[2] (cf. Noreen, Gr., § 244. a. 2).

   e) in other cases as follows: *tan* 37 (cf. *tua* 6[2], 13[x], 111[11], forms of *vard(v)acita* 4 t. *c.g.* 15[7] ∼ *v* 8 t., forms of *rdarr* 8[9], 63[2] (∼ *v* 15[15]).

§ 51. *uu* ' *gg* in *binggnz* 61[2].

CHAPTER V

INSERTION OF CONSONANTS.

§ 52. **Insertion of** *t* occurs as follows:

   1) between *ll* and *s*; *allz* 5 t. *c.g.* 84[6], *gullz* 4 t. *c.g.* 62[11], *mikillz* 81[13] (cf. *mikils* 4 t. *c.g.* 33[10]), *pellz* 73[13], *spen(n)zl* 86[14], -*tiallz* 99[7], *vallz* 7[8], 81[3], forms of *aellztr* 38[8], 78[15].

   2) between *nn'n* and *s*; *man(n)z* 81[1] (cf. -*manz* 61[10]), *minzta* 38[9].

   3) in the gen. sg., where *s* alone is regular, as follows: *enskiz* 81[1] (perhaps dittography. It is followed by *mannz*), *landz* 3 t. *c.g.* 17[10], *lam(n)z* 20[3], *profastz* 23[10], *vatz* 61[6], *hetz* 3 t. (cf. *ts* 104[x]).

   4) in the interior of a word; in forms of *bacizl* with *zl* 3 t. 62[14], 108[12], 111[14] (cf. *sl* 5 t *c.g.* 32[4]).

   5) before *z*, in *vacitzlu* 2[10] (cf. *vacizlu* 6[x], 99[16]), *hetza* 10[6], 73[11] (cf. forms with *zt* m. t.).

3

6) In superlatives, where *ts* appears instead of *st*.

huitazta 73[14], *kacraztu* 8[4], *saurgazti* 105[8], *skiotazt* 13 t. e. g. 100[13] (∼ *st* 4 t. e. g. 24[3]), *soemilegazt* 84[11], *vapnfimazti* 108[3].

The reason for *z* in the superlative is not clear. Cf. Hom. Ll., p. 118, Noreen, Gr., § 247, a. 4.

7) *z* in the medio-passive.

The regular ending for the reflexive at this period is *z* for all forms. The endings which occur in El. are as follows:

Infinitive, *z* 34 t. ∼ *tz* 3 t. in *heriatz* 36[6], *komatz* 37[9], 73[5]; -*sk* once, in *komask* 96[2]; -*zk* twice in *firrazk* 22[5], *lucazk* 62[4].

1st sg. pres., *mz* 11 t. e. g. *naudgumz* 88[3].

2nd sg. pres., *z* 2 t. e. g. *sigraz* 82[5] ∼ *zt* once, in *haetazt* 109[11], *zk* once, in *sezk* 61[9].

3rd sg. pres., *z* 16 t. e. g. *nalgaz* 35[2] ∼ *sk* once, in *bersc* 92[7].

1st pl. pr., *mz* 3 t. e. g. *skiliumz* 25[3].

2nd pl. pr., *z* 3 t. e. g. *buiz* 85[13].

3rd pl. pr., *z* 11 t. e. g. *kallaz* 9[7] ∼ *zt* once in *haettazt* 72[2]. Imp. pr., *z* 7 t. e. g. *raez* 37[14] ∼ *sk* once in *bersk* 100[13], *zk* once, in *raezk* 85[4].

1st sg. pt., *mz* 5 t. e. g. *dueldumz* 14[10].

3rd sg. pt., *z* 61 t. e. g. *knaz* 78[8] ∼ *zk* twice in *letzk* 82[1] (cf. *laetk* 81[6] *s* lost), *skauzk* 68 [8].

3rd pl. pt., *z* 17 t. e. g. *bingguz* 61[2] ∼ *zt* twice, *sloguzt* 43[3], *villtuzt* 68[1].

ppl., *z* 7 t. *tekiz* 43[9] ∼ *zk* 3 t. *girn(n)zk* 90[4], *huillzk* 13[5], *vardzk* 44[16].

From the above list of forms it will be seen that *tz* occurs twice; *zk* 9 times; *sk* 3 times; — the two latter are unusual in Norwegian mss. — *zt* 4 times and is followed in every case by *þ*; *hacitazt þu* 109[11], *haettazt þeir* 72[2], *sloguzt þegar* 43[3], *villtuzt þeir* 68[1].

§ 53. **Insertion of *þ*** — from cases where *þ* originally preceded. *þit* (pers. pron.) 42[8], 73[5], *þer* (pl.) m. t. e. g. 68[8]. Cf. Noreen, Gr., § 394, a, 5.

§ 54. **Insertion of r.** *haverska* 22[1] cf. *har(er)sc laciks* 1[x], *haverk lacik* 86[1].

r is added in *hestr* 35[11] (a. s.), or it might rather be regarded as the nom. case used for the acc.

§ 55. **Insertion of i.** These cases have been treated under palatal *g* and *k*.

Proper Names.

Since the Norwegian and French versions vary considerably in respect to the proper names, it is, in most cases, impossible to decide what name stood in the original. This is especially true in the case of the numerous names inserted in the Norwegian version, which the French text does not show at all. Of the names occurring several times, some of the more important variations in writing are as follows:

Aemers 15[8] = *Aimar* 77[3], *Agamore* 77[2] = *Agamers* 15[13], *-mrs* 15[x], *Aernalld* 18[10] = *Arnalld* 24[15], 39[12], *Bertram* 21[11], (m) 20[6], 24[14] = *Bertramn* 18[9], 32[5], *-fn* 39[7], another instance of the confusion of *mn/fn* in this dialect, cf. p. 18. *Kaifas* 8 t. e. g. 80[11] = *Kaifass* 80[13], *Karlla magnus* 48 shows *ll* after *r* (cf. p. 27). *Cursant* 21[1] = *Kursot* 25[7] (C) 26[1]. *Dionisij*, (*Denis*), 2[5], 17[3], *Egidij* (*Gille*), 5 t. e. g. 12[10], *Hylarij* 3[10] are the only examples of -*ij* for the Latin genitive.

In *Elena* 101[6] initial H is dropped, also in *Ertun* 68[12] = *Hertori* 65[13], *-tur* 66[12]. The name *Loeys* (*Ludwig*) found in the Fr. ms. occurs in two cases: *Laeyuisi* 4[x], *Loevisi* 17[12]. *Je(su)s Chr(istu)s* 31[16] bis, (cf. *Je(su)s Kristr* 7[11]) is one of the three instances of *Ch* in the ms. The others are: *Malchabrie* 20[12], and *Chiatres* 5[x]. *Josi* 12 t. e. g. 20[1] = *Jose* 41[3], 102[12] and *Jasi* 42[6], *Josiar* 31[10]. *Julien* occurs m. t. e. g. 78[1] where the Fr. has *Jubien*. The name written *Mahomet* in the Fr. shows great variation in the guttural: *Mahun* 25[10], *Magun* 7 t. (acct. *un* 89[12]), *Maghun* 26 t. (-*un* 59[11]), *Mahgun* 27[6], also *Maumet* 20[2], 99[16]. *Salatre* 4 t. e. g. 10[9] = *Malatries* 27[5], *-rer* 30[1,x], *-ren* a. s. 29[9], 31[10]. These names are confused in the Fr. also. *Malkabres* varies in the ending: *-bres* 19[9], 69[12], *-brez* 7 t. e. g. 20[1], (cf. *Malchabriez* 20[12]), *-bre* 8 t. e. g. 43[10] (cf. *le* 102[10]), *Malscabre* 114[3,11]. *Ozible* 3 = *Olive* in the Fr. *Paris* 101[8] occurs with accent *Páris* 101[5], *Rodeant* 21[1]

Rodean 22^8, 23^3, *Rodoan* 25^7, 26^1. *Rosamunda* has gen. in
-*ar* c. g. 102^4, acc. in -*am* c. g. 72^3. *Tiatres* 4 t. c. g. 20^{14} =
Triatres 28^{10}. The forms of *l'Iliamr* are regular c. g. 21^{13}.
The initial is written *U* 38^9, 39^2. *Alexandria* 5 t. c. g. 42^6 =
-*dre* 41^1, cf. *Arabia hestr* 67^{10}, 109^{11}, -*ie* 17^{14}. *Iragunt* 3 t.
c. g. 34^7 · *Iragnn* 3 t. c. g. 92^5. The following variations
in the name *France*: *Fraclande* 91^7, (*k*) 96^8; *Franz* 30^8, *n(n)z*
5 t. c. g. 38^3, *Fracka k(onnn)gs* 1^4 cf. *Franka* 76^{15}, *Frankis*
in composition with forms of *madr* 8 t. c.g. 27^{12}. *Oraengi borg*
20^6 = *Orengi borg* 8 t. c. g. 39^3. *Troia* 101^5 cf. *Troe* 101^9.

www.ingramcontent.com/pod-product-compliance
Lightning Source LLC
Chambersburg PA
CBHW021549270326
41930CB00008B/1434